YOUR LOGBOOK:

GOD AS AN ARTIST

49 ACTIVATIONS FOR YOUR OWN

CREATIVITY

Jörn Lange

Also by Jörn Lange

Intercession through Creative Expression—Drawing Heaven to Earth in the Creative Flow

Biblical Foundations of Prophetic Art—Finding Keys in Scripture

Dein Logbuch: Gott als Künstler—49 Impulse für die eigene Kreativität

Bist' nicht von Hier? Mai bis August 1945—Rückweg ins Ungewisse nach einer wahren Geschichte

ISBN: 9789925772544

A copy of this title is held at the Cyprus Library.

YOUR LOGBOOK:
GOD AS AN ARTIST

49 Activations for Your Own Creativity

Jörn Lange

ACKNOWLEDGEMENTS

I want to thank the Lord for encouraging me to write this book, guiding me through the entire process. I am grateful to my wife, Sheila, who has stood behind me and my many projects over the years.

Thank you to the friends who offered suggestions, encouragement, and prayers for me as I wrote. I want to mention in particular Manuela Blocher, Hanne Cullingford, Birgit Hämmerle, Dr. Ute Horn, Janey Pettersen, Gregor and Waltraud Pircher, and Rudi Töws, some of whom also did the proof reading. Their trust in me and their confidence helped me to keep going through the difficult times.

I am indebted to the leader of my mission agency in Germany, Andreas Pestke, who welcomed me writing a third book and encouraged me to take the time to write it.

I really appreciate you all!

Table of Contents

HOW THIS BOOK CAME ABOUT

Ever since I came to understand that I am made in the image of the ultimate artist, I have wondered about God as an artist. At the beginning of the second lock down in Cyprus in the autumn of 2020. I was again confronted with a period of time that was very frustrating because, due to the restrictions, I could not meet people and paint prophetically for them. I had already done a lot of research on the topic of "God as an artist." Then one Saturday morning, I felt inspired to work on the subject further and, to my surprise, I began to write this book in German.

A number of my friends read the first versions of the text and made suggestions. It became clear that I was composing a logbook with activations for creativity. The text went through many changes and was finally translated into English. I hope that the readers of this book experience the changes that God will bring about in them as they apply the activations in this book to their own creativity and artistic expression: changes that will lead to new perspectives and experiences.

God as an artist and we as artists. When I write "artist," I use this term in an all-encompassing way regardless of the creative means or forms of expression and the techniques which someone uses. Musicians, songwriters, poets, singers, sculptors, painters, potters, carpenters, photographers, filmmakers, goldsmiths, designers, and others can all be artists and all prophetic.

A few words on the subject of the logbook. A log was originally a piece of wood on a line that was used to calculate the speed of ships. In connection with the course, which was determined by the use of a compass, it was possible to determine the location of the ship. The speed and the location of the ship, as well as events that were important were then entered into the logbook. The Bible is our log. The logbook that you are holding in your hands can help you to determine your own course and location. We will refer to a number of scriptures that show us God as an artist. All the scripture messages lead to 49 creative activations that will help you to understand your own creativity better. You can implement these activations in your own form of creative expression and use the appropriate means, such as a sketchbook, a writing pad, sheet music or a type setting programme.

Those who held responsibility kept a logbook. On warships the logbook wa kept by the officers on watch and on merchant ships, it was kept by the helmsmen. God invites you to take responsibility for your creative calling. With this logbook, He gives you the competence to accomplish that purpose.

49 CREATIVE ACTIVATIONS

There are countless suggestions in the scriptures related to art. Step-by-step, the various aspects of God's artistic expression are put into words that give you wings. They are not meant to overwhelm you but to give you a view of your world from above, with space to articulate, depict and understand your thoughts, revelations, and answers. The Scriptures also afford you an opportunity to confront and resolve your challenges, fears and worries. Creative activations are tools to help your heart and your understanding of your own creativity. They are suggestions to examine thoughts that you may not have allowed yourself to think, to visualise, to write, to paint, to dance, or to express as your own creative statements. You may also experience challenges and encouragements to take your preferred creative language seriously and to freely apply what you learn.

Why 49? While I was reading through the original draft of this book to see where such activations could be added to the text, I came across 49 places. That is the simple explanation. 49 is also seven times seven. Seven is the number of perfection in the Bible. In Matthew 5:48, we are challenged to be perfect like our Heavenly Father. The word that is translated here as perfect is the Greek word teleios. Its root meaning is to set yourself in motion with a specific goal. The purpose of this book is to encourage you to set yourself in motion with a specific goal.

DO YOU HAVE A GOAL?

Allow yourself to have a goal! Why do you want to read this logbook and implement the activations?

To gain more confidence in your own creativity?

To have more joy?

To learn to listen more to God?

To deprive fears and rejections of their power?

To overcome false beliefs that keep you down?

Formulate your goal. It may challenge you. Please write it down so that you keep it in mind.

Set up a "no matter what" place where, with the material containing your creative expression, you can read, think, and be creative without being disturbed. It can be a comfortable armchair, an art studio, a dance floor, or a pottery wheel. Select a setting that encourages you to be creative. Coffee or music might also help. Include anything that helps you to direct your personal attention to God and to your own creativity.

Have fun doing it. The activations are not classes that should be worked through. Rather, they are invitations to know God and yourself better as you grow deeper into your own calling, with joy.

Give God space! Become still, listen to Him, let Him speak His peace to you, before reading a section. Digest it, let it sink in and devote yourself to the respective activation. And then: CAST OFF!

Jörn Lange

INTRODUCTION

God as an artist? Sunsets and the diversity of creation come to mind. A God who sings and makes music? A God who tells stories? Who designs gardens and plants wine? Who makes pottery? Who might dance Himself? Who plans art, clothing, and buildings? There is much to suggest that God as an artist makes use of a number of forms of expression that we tend not to notice in Scripture, or have merely overlooked so far. What does this have to do with creativity? If God is such a multifaceted artist, then all artists have both feet firmly in the character of the Creator. They all receive their creativity, their modes of expression, their identity and their legitimacy, from Him: the ultimate artist. His character is His motivation. What is ours?

How God expresses Himself and what that has to do with us, are shown to us by eight artistic forms of expression that flow out of His character. In characterizing these forms of expression, I rely on the original texts of the Scriptures. I am not a theologian, so I use available specialised literature to explore the original meanings of the respective terms that can help us understand the character of God. I have deliberately omitted footnotes and cite my main source, Strong's Concordance, with Hebrew and Greek Lexicons in brackets after the word meanings, in case someone wants to dig deeper (e.g. G2307). To explain the root meanings that Strong translated into English, I also used German, Dutch, and Spanish translations. The more deeply I studied the meanings of the terms in the original languages, the clearer it became to me that many phrases can only be reproduced by one word in a fluent and easily readable translation, but they contain a more complex meaning we can discover.

Sometimes I felt like an archaeologist looking into the original texts (not that I studied archaeology or ancient history.) Neither did I study Hebrew or ancient Greek. But just as someone can go to an archaeological excavation and read the information boards in order to understand what one is seeing, one can also approach the original text with the appropriate aids and use the published knowledge of experts to understand what scholars have already researched.

As a child, I always admired the complex masterpieces that one could buy in the pastry shops of my hometown. These cakes presented the art and skills of the confectioner in an impressive way. I like to think back to Bavarian layer cake and gooseberry meringue or eggnog cake. They had multiple layers, the more the better. You did not stay at the surface of the cake, which looks nice, and possibly quite uniform, but you cut the cake and then enjoyed it layer by layer, or in cross section, seeing all the details at the same time. I hope that you will discover the complex topics of this book layer by layer, but also see all the details at the same time, in their complexity.

CHAPTER 1: GOD CREATES

GOD'S MOTIVATION

"In the beginning, Elohim created the heavens and the earth. And Elohim said: let us make people in our own image (Gen. 1:1 and 1:26)."

Elohim, the first word for God we see in Scripture, is the Israelites' word for "God." It describes the Creator and distinguishes Him from idols that are not to be worshipped. It is written in the plural, as God is plural.

The character of God is multi-perspective, comprehensive, and unrestricted in every aspect so that God cannot be described in the singular. Not limited. He creates from the fullness of Himself, and He is absolute, self-motivated, and full of imagination

.What Motivates Him To Create?

"Worthy are You, our Lord and God, to receive the glory and the honour and the power; for You created all things, and because of Your will they exist, and were created and brought into being" (Rev. 4:11.)

Elohim wanted the world—a simple statement that is not complex. "Will" is translated from the Greek word thelema (G2307). This word describes a decision, a calling, a commandment, a purpose, and a joy—a word with many facets and meanings. God creates through His will and out of His joy. He gives what is created both a meaning and a purpose. There is a lot for us to discover including His joy. God has joy. He is excited, enthusiastic and pleased. He is not an impersonal or absent ruler. He invites us, through His son, the incarnate person of Himself, to become His friends (John 15:15) and to participate in His creation.

We become His friends when we do what He entrusts us to do (John 15:14). He entrusts us with His will, His purposes, and His intentions for us. He trusts us to manage well with what we have received from Him (Matt 25:14) and to act according to His will. Jesus gives us the power to do what is God's will as well as what pleases Him (Heb. 13:21). We can recognise His will, His creative pleasure, which is good and perfect, because Jesus re-orients all our thinking (Rom 12:2) by filling us with wisdom and insight (Col. 1:9). In His joy, there is wisdom and insight of the Creator with which we can be filled. God fills our cup again and again with his joy and His Spirit.

ACTIVATION 1:

YOUR MOTIVATION

God has a motivation. He creates out of joy, calls us and instructs us to do the same. I invite you to answer the following questions: What is your motivation? What is your incentive for being creative? Have you received a commission from God, or is your creativity the result of a longer process, or is it both? Do you share God's joy when you are creative, and if so, how is this joy expressed? If not, do you have any idea what could be the problem? Who or what is in your way? With regard to your creativity, is your thinking completely focussed on God, His order, His will, and His joy?

Take the time to pray about and to answer some or all of these questions. Express your answers in your own creative language.

God's Purpose:

If we look at what Jesus wants, we see that He behaves exactly like His father:

As He said, "I do not seek My own will, but only the will of Him who sent me" (John 5:30).

The result of the realisation of this inspiring, joyful, and joy-giving will is a network of purposeful relationships.

As Jesus reminds us, "Whoever does what my Father in heaven wants, that person is my brother and sister and mother" (Matt. 12:50. CJB).

Obedience to the Father is the foundation for a joyful family that has meaning and a purpose.

ACTIVATION 2:

BEING A FAMILY

As previously quoted, Jesus taught that: "Whoever does what my Father in heaven wants, that person is my brother and sister and mother" (Matt. 12:50. CJB).

Do you experience this new family in the body of Christ, in the local church, or with other artists? Jesus said that when we do His will, we experience real fellowship on very different levels, with other disciples and other artists. What can you do to change any negative experiences in this family or to expand on positive ones?

Take the time to pray about and to answer some or all of these questions. Express your answers in your own creative language.

Creativity Is God's Heart

What Elohim intends when He creates in His will is to give calling, meaning, joy, and works of art that find the highest expression in people (Gen. 1:26-27). His creativity and innovative power are not merely some of His personal characteristics, but the heart of His personality, His heart that He shows us.

Creativity In The Bible

It is revealing to see that the word creativity is not used in the Bible. Nowhere in scripture do we find a single noun that would define the concept of creativity. The fullness of God is at the heart of His personality and cannot be ultimately defined, limited, or fixed. God's creativity is not a theory, but rather it shows itself in action. This is an important contrast because God's creativity is shown through action, service, initiative, and results. Even where the biblical text says "creator," that is, where the translation uses a noun, the original text often contains a verb or a phrase that describes action, not merely a single "thing word." The creator in Romans 1:25 is literally "the one who created." In Job 36:3, the creator is literally "making"—merely someone who is about to do something.

God's creative action is open to us. He invites us to participate (Gen. 1:26-27). He calls on us to actively dive into the flow of His life and to participate in His action in an effervescent, lively, alert, and committed manner. When we participate in His actions, they become our good works in which we are to walk (Eph. 2:10). He puts us in this state through His actions. He is an active God who creates, gives meaning to our lives, and draws us into His family, if we let Him.

ACTIVATION 3:

CREATIVITY IS ACTION

Is this statement unusual and new? How do you feel about creativity? I have heard many times that creativity is like a tank that you can tap into. You just have to find your way into the tank in the right way. However, I do not find this way of thinking in the Bible. What does it mean for you that creativity is not a concept, but an invitation to action? An invitation into the river of God or an invitation to take a risk?

Take the time to pray about and to answer some or all of these questions. Express your answers in your own creative language.

Diverse Creation

If you want to read more about God's creative work, you can look at Psalm 104. It contains 35 verses filled with God's actions. Not a single concept, but numerous actions to show why God deserves praise. Creating is action and shows how God takes the initiative. God is the one who creates everything, who determines effects and grants provision to us. Psalm 104 describes many interactions that God planned with foresight, and all of these actions lead us to praise Him.

As Isa. 45:18a describes, God acts as a creator in three different ways:

It is written, "For thus says Adonai who created the heavens, God, who shaped and made the earth, who established it and created it not to be chaos, but formed it to be lived in" (CJB).

"Created" in Hebrew is bara, which is also used in Genesis 1:2 (H1254). "Shaped" is the Hebrew word yatsar, which refers to the work of a potter who presses clay into a mould (H3335). "Established" is the Hebrew word kun (H3559), which can mean standing, setting up, founding, building, steering, directing, consecrating and providing, among other things. "Formed" is the Hebrew word yatsar again.

In the well-known Psalm 139, God's creative work is compared, for example, to weaving. In verse 13 it says:

"You wove me in my mother's womb" (NASB).

The Hebrew word sakak is translated here as "wove" (H5526). The root meaning of this verb is to loop around or to curl. In verse 15 it says:

"I was intricately and skilfully formed [as if being embroidered with many colours] in the depths of the earth" (AMP).

The Hebrew word raqam is translated as "embroidered" (7551). Its root meaning describes varying colours. This verb was used to describe the activities of embroidering, stitching or knitting with multiple colours. God's creative acts are so wonderfully complex as He varies the colours in His joy and weaves us according to His pattern—Himself. His creative acts are complete to the last detail, artfully ingenious and diverse.

ACTIVATION 4:

GOD IS ACTIVE

Please read the biblical passages recorded in Psalm 104, Isaiah 45:18, and Psalm 139:13-15. I suggest that you write down the verbs in these scriptures and also refer to various English translations of them. All of these verbs show an aspect of God's creativity in action. Now choose a few that appeal to you in particular and determine: what do they mean to you?

Take the time to pray about and to answer some or all of these questions. Express your answers in your own creative language.

The Meaning And Beauty Of Creation

We also see diversity when we look at the result of God's action: creation. It is the expression of a happy artist who gives meaning to life. Meaning that is not only expressed in being useful but unfolds in beauty. People are often shaped by logical thinking and ask about the meaning, purpose, and use of something or even a person. But God not only creates to fulfil a purpose or to create something useful, He also creates to develop beauty and to enjoy it. We too can enjoy His creation. An abundance of verses in the Bible describe the beauty of creation and what it tells us about the creator. Psalm 19:1-4a tells us:

> The heavens declare the glory of God; the skies proclaim the work of his hands.
>
> Day after day they pour forth speech; night after night they reveal knowledge.
>
> They have no speech, they use no words; no sound is heard from them.
>
> Yet their voice goes out into all the earth, their words to the ends of the world. (NIV)
>
> At the end of the Psalm, David asks,
>
> "May these words of my mouth and this meditation of my heart be pleasing in your sight, Lord, my Rock and my Redeemer." (NIV)

The word "acceptable" is translated from the Hebrew word ratson (H7522), which corresponds to the Greek thelema, which is translated as will or joy in Revelation 4:11. The beauty of creation leads the viewer to behave in a pleasing manner, and to live in the will of God, which I find fascinating.

It has been said many times that God wrote two books. The first one is the Bible, the written book in which He communicates Himself to us. The second book is creation. It shows Him unmistakably as the Creator. Let us think of the splendour of the colours in animals, the ability of some to camouflage themselves or to deceive their enemies by their appearance, such as insects that look like leaves. The grandeur of colours in plants that Jesus spoke about (Luke 12:27); orchids that look like monkeys (Dracula simia) or like flying ducks (Caleana major); plants that disguise themselves as stones (lithops) and much more. Is everything functional and useful? Not at all, but some are an expression of the playful joy that the Creator had in creating the world.

ACTIVATION 5:

BEAUTY VERSUS UTILITY

Creation fulfils a purpose in that one part of creation often benefits from another. On the other hand, creation also makes the beauty of God's work a reality. When you look at your creativity or your art, do you see the fulfilment of usefulness that is expressed in the purpose of a work of art, or do you see the development of beauty? It can and should be both at the same time.

Take the time to pray about and to answer some or all of these questions. Express your answers in your own creative language.

Exuberant Beauty

Two further examples should be sufficient to illustrate this playful beauty that is visible in God's loving actions. Jesus tells His listeners that they need not worry because not even Solomon in all his splendour was dressed like one of these lilies of the field (Matt. 6:29).

Lilies have always been an eye-catcher. The concept that lead Jesus to speak of the lilies of the field is that God has so much to give, He even dresses flowers—that are going to be thrown in the fire—so exuberantly, and elegantly (verse 30). His resources, available to us, are inexhaustible. Thus, listeners can expect that God will give much more to us than to the lilies, as we are made in the image of God. The lilies do not struggle and can neither spin nor weave. The exuberant provision for the lilies does not depend on their efforts or their abilities, but instead it depends on God's loving actions.

God places His rainbow in the sky, which reflects all the colours of sunlight in its radial colour gradient, as a sign of the covenant with humanity (Gen. 9:8-17). The beauty of the rainbow makes the viewer aware of God's promise of His covenant. God reminds us with this symbol of His promises, as well as with His faithfulness, to the people and to each individual. The rainbow is created when opposites—sun and rain—collide and seemingly could not coexist. In the same way, God gives us such reconciliation by not accounting for our sins and by forgiving us. This covenant promise, which was fulfilled on the cross, is embodied in the rainbow which symbolises the resolution between two opposites. Again, the beauty of creation makes a statement about the Creator who is the Alpha and Omega of His creation.

As noted by Paul, the people have always been able to see and experience His eternal power and divine majesty in His works, the creation (Rom. 1:20).

ACTIVATION 6:

BEAUTY FOR YOU

When you look at the lilies of the field that flourish today and will be thrown into the fire tomorrow, do you think of lavishness and generosity, like a fruit tree in the spring that is covered over and over with blossoms? God gives His beauty generously because He has more than enough of it. He gives it to you and to me. What do you receive from His beauty as a person and as an artist? Do you receive through your own efforts and ability or as a gift from God's hand? God's covenant promises to squander Himself on us to show us God's faithfulness. Are you experiencing this as a person and as an artist?

Take the time to pray about and to answer some or all of these questions. Express your answers in your own creative language.

The Beauty Of God

The beauty of God Himself, the beauty of the ultimate and original artist, is also extensively described in the Bible. The Israelites experienced Him as a pillar of cloud by day and a pillar of fire by night (Ex 13:21). What an awesome sight! Think of photographs of clouds in the desert or of pillars of fire. Today we try to tame towers of fire for coziness in the garden, but the pillar of fire in the desert was not tame and gentle, but instead, majestic and extraordinary. The pillar of cloud showed God's protection during the day. It provided shade against the heat of the desert and gave moisture to relieve the parchedness. The pillar of fire in the night gave warmth in the cold and gave light and direction.

In Daniel 7:9-10, God's clothing

"was white as snow,
And the hair of his head like pure wool.

His throne was ablaze with flames,
Its wheels were a burning fire.

A river of fire was flowing
And coming out from before him" (NASB).

Once again, we have a majestic, awe-inspiring and powerful description of the appearance of God. We find a similar description of God's beauty in Ezekiel 1:26-28:

"Now above the expanse that was over their heads there was something resembling a throne, like lapis lazuli in appearance; and on that which resembled a throne, high up, was a figure with the appearance of a man. Then I noticed from the appearance of His waist and upward something like gleaming metal that looked like fire all around within it, and from the appearance of His waist and downwards.

I saw something like fire, and there was a radiance around Him. Like the appearance of the rainbow in the clouds on a rainy day, so was the appearance of the surrounding radiance. Such was the appearance of the likeness of the glory of the LORD. And when I saw it, I fell on my face" (NASB).

In Revelation 4:2-3 again we read,

> "Immediately I was in the Spirit; and behold, a throne was standing in heaven, and someone was sitting on the throne. And He who was sitting was like a jasper stone and a sardius in appearance; and there was a rainbow around the throne, like an emerald in appearance" (NASB).

That is a beauty as radiant as if you were looking into an active volcano.

We can see that both Ezekiel and John lacked words to accurately describe what they saw. The beauty of God is so breath-taking, so unique, grandiose, overwhelming, and incomparable that it is beyond the scope of human imagination and depiction. Such is the Creator whom we can experience as artists.

ACTIVATION 7:

AWESOME BEAUTY

We have seen that the writers of the Bible describe the intrusion of God's beauty into their reality as fire. You see the rainbow in all its colours in the shimmering light of the person of Jesus, who is probably described in Ezekiel, and around the throne of God in Revelation. The beauty of God speaks to us through awe, warmth, protection, and direction.

Do you experience awe when you deal with the beauty of God? When you encounter it in reality or when you are being creative and examining your art at the end of a creative process? Do you instead doubt yourself and question whether what you are doing has something to do with God? As human beings, we often deal with a laboriousness factor because our abilities may not accurately represent the idea we have in mind, and there is still room for improvement.

Take the time to pray about and to answer some or all of these questions. Express your answers in your own creative language.

Jesus As Creator

How is Jesus also the creator? Can the Creator be only a single divinity? The Bible describes this in many ways. However, if the Creator is already described in the plural in the first verse of Scripture, then we can understand this apparent contradiction at least to the extent that Jesus is the Creator already laid out in God's plurality. Jesus did not stand idly by or look on passively in creation. Paul explains this apparent contradiction in 1 Corinthians 8:6 by teaching that;

"Yet for us there is only one God, the Father, from whom are all things, and we exist for Him; and one Lord, Jesus Christ, by whom are all things, and we exist through Him" (NASB).

Paul says that the Father is the one who created everything, and at the same time, that Jesus is the one through whom everything was created.

It is astonishing that there is not a single verb in the original Greek text! "Are" and "exist" do not appear in the original. The interlinear translations say: "One God, the Father, from whom everything and we to him, and one Lord, Jesus Christ, through whom everything and we through him." It is that simple. Or not. Paul touches upon the act of creation by explicitly omitting it, which speaks volumes. Jesus is the one through whom everything is created, exists, has its form and value, receives its purposes, and experiences its meaning. We are also created through Him, exist through Him, receive our form through Him, experience our worth, and live through Him in our destiny. Our lives make sense through Him, but nevertheless, we are created by the Father.

In Colossians 1:15, Paul describes this connection, interrelation, and covenant between Father and Son as Creator by portraying Jesus as the image of God. Paul then writes that through Him, the image, everything is created, and that through Him, God's likeness, everything will finally be completed (Col 1:17). Here Paul describes Jesus as the starting point and the end point of all creation and as all-encompassing. At the end of the Greek text in verse 16, it says that all things were created "for Him." The word translated "for" is the Greek word eis (G1519). It can also mean in favour of, for the sake of or with intention towards. It expresses a goal, and when used with a verb in this case "created" describes an action.

ACTIVATION 8:

YOU THROUGH HIM

We are included in this covenant and in this goal. "We through Him" is a concise statement. What does this mean for you as an artist? "You through Him." Please take some time to be still before God and ask Him what this means. Is your art the work of your heart? Is your art aimed at Him? How does He work through your art? Does He speak to you through your art? Does He speak to others through your art?

> Take the time to pray about and to answer some or all of these questions. Express your answers in your own creative language.

The Importance Of Every Life

Peter says the same thing to the Jews in the Temple. In Acts 3:15, he preaches that all life comes from Jesus, the "originator of life." This includes the life that was created at the beginning—every life, regardless of the human templates into which we try to squeeze it. This applies whether someone is an artist or not. The categories we invent to create differences sometimes seem to be infinite. Every life comes from Jesus, the Creator and artist. We may have to take a deep breath and let that sink in.

ACTIVATION 9:

DISTORTED TEMPLATES

Which templates—which categories—which type of blinders do we wear? When you look at your own life, do you see that it comes from Jesus? Are there other lives that you look at, or other people you meet, where you find it difficult to accept or perceive that their life also comes from Jesus? In some cases, a life may reflect more of the fall of man than the origin—the joy of God. What can you do to step out of the templates that you may perceive and recognise the origin of life in others?

> Take the time to pray about and to answer some or all of these questions. Express your answers in your own creative language.

Jesus As The Origin

In Revelation 3:14, John records a statement Jesus made about Himself. Jesus calls Himself the origin of all that God created. The origin is the cause and the causer of all that God created. Jesus formulates His connection with the Father in the creation process very clearly at the end of the Bible. "Origin" here is the translation of the Greek word arche (G746). It is used over 50 times in the New Testament and can also mean cause, power, principle, commandment or standard, in various places. This gives us an idea of what Jesus was talking about when He names Himself as arche.

ACTIVATION 10:

BACK TO THE ORIGIN

Do we see Jesus as the origin, the cause, and the standard in our creative work? Is Jesus, His behaviour, His messages, His invitations to you, His statements about you, and His lifestyle the measuring line you use when you receive inspiration? Are you inspired by Him when you paint, dance, sculpt, write, sing, or work with fabrics? This is often not a simple inquiry. Go deeper into these questions to find out in prayer, and in silence, to what degree and in what ways you make Jesus the source of your inspiration and creativity.

> Take the time to pray about and to answer some or all of these questions. Express your answers in your own creative language.

The New Creation

What I find particularly fascinating in this connection between Father and Son is that through Jesus, we can clearly see that God continues to create today. The New Testament often speaks of the "new creation" and the "new creature." Second Corinthians 5:17 shows us the basic prerequisite for this event where it is written that:

> "Therefore if anyone is in Christ, this person is a new creation [or creature]" (NASB).

The interlinear translation similarly provides:

> "When someone in Christ, a new creation [or creature]."

Again, a sentence without a verb in the original text that is a description of the new situation, a characterisation of the quality, the constitution in which someone is "who (is) in Christ." The Greek word en (G1722) is a preposition that describes several things, including a fixed position, being a tool for someone, a relationship of calm, or of silence between two things or people. One suggested translation in the original English version of Strong's Concordance is: "To give oneself completely to someone or something."

Jesus as Creator does not give us something back that was lost through the fall all but creates something new, and fresh—something that did not exist before. That is one reason why we are named in James 1:18 as "first fruits" of His new creation, alluding to the Old Testament sacrificial system. This also shows that the new creation, through Jesus, is inherent in our destiny as a living sacrifice (Rom 12:1). The first fruits are those offered as a sacrifice to God and not available to anyone to fulfil his or her own needs. This sacrifice originally expressed the confidence that God will give all the abundance of the harvest, even after the first fruits.

ACTIVATION 11:

THE NEW CREATURE

Does the "new creature" describe your condition always, and everywhere, and in every situation? Do you allow yourself to be made into a tool for Jesus in your art? Do you have a relationship of rest, of stillness, and of peace with Jesus? What does it mean for you as an artist, as a new creature of the Creator, and to offer your life as a living sacrifice?

Take the time to pray about and to answer some or all of these questions. Express your answers in your own creative language.

Here And Now

The new creation expresses itself in two areas. On the one hand in the here and now, since we become new people in our earthly, current, daily reality. On the other hand, in the future, since at the end of the now, a new heaven and a new earth will come (Isa. 65:17, 2 Pet. 3:13, Rev. 21:1). As prophetic artists, we live in the here and now in our everyday lives. How does the emergence of the new creature take place? In Colossians 3:9-10, Paul writes that we stripped off the old life like old clothes and put on new clothes because we are new people. New clothes of beauty like the robes of the lilies in the field (Matt. 6:28). God's fullness in us—now.

In the here and now, God is constantly at work in us so that we can conform more and more to His image in which He created us. This reference back to Genesis 1:26-27 shows us the revolutionary nature of this new creation. Jesus as Creator does not remove shortcomings, dirt, and vice from us in order to clean us up and make us presentable. He creates someone completely new, so new that the reference back to the original imago Dei, the untouched likeness, is justified. We will be like those who dream (Ps. 126:1).

In Ephesians 4:24, we clearly read that the new man is "in the likeness of God" (NASB) or "to be godly" (CJB). "In the likeness" is the Greek preposition kata (G2596). It has a wealth of meanings. One could also translate the new person as "related to God" or "created in God's being." Saying that the new human being was created "in the manner of God" would also work. This miracle is as amazing as the first creation by Father and Son, God-like in his character, and in his likeness. As Vincent van Gogh once said, Jesus was, "an artist, greater than all other artists." C. S. Lewis wrote: "God became man to turn creatures into sons: not simply to produce better men of the old kind but to produce a new kind of man. It is not like teaching a horse to jump better and better but like turning a horse into a winged creature."

ACTIVATION 12:

EXPERIENCE OF ABUNDANCE

God's fullness in us. Is that your experience? When is that your experience? Are you practicing God's abundance in you? Does the experience of abundance, and the experience of the presence of God in your inspiration and in your art, depend on your external circumstances? Do you experience yourself as a winged creature or as a better jumping horse?

> Take the time to pray about and to answer some or all of these questions. Express your answers in your own creative language.

CHAPTER 2:

GOD RAISES HIS VOICE

The first art form that God uses in the Bible is His voice. He speaks creation into existence. A look at Genesis 1 shows us eleven times when God speaks something into existence. He speaks into existence, and He names things such as day and night in verse five or heaven and earth in verses eight and ten. In Ezekiel 12:25 we see exactly that what He says happens:

> "For I the Lord will speak whatever word I speak, and it will be performed. It will no longer be delayed, for in your days, you rebellious house, I will speak the word and perform it, declares the Lord" (NASB).

God Himself speaks about His "word," dabar in Hebrew (H1697), which has two basic meanings we in the West often neatly separate: dabar comprises the word itself and the deed that puts the word into action!

In the New Testament we find something similar in James 1:18, where it says that

"He gave us birth by the word of truth" (NASB).

The Greek expression, translated here as "word" is logos. God has the right word at the right time; His word in His timing. He takes it and puts it into action. From the beginning.

ACTIVATION 13:

GOD'S VOICE

Are You Familiar With God's Voice?

Take some time and think about how God speaks to you. How do you experience the voice of God? Some people hear it as an inner voice; acquaintances and friends speak into our lives; fellow Christians give us prophetic words that confirm things God has shown us; a word from the Bible seems to catch our eye; God gives us peace in our hearts to make a certain decision. Now and then people hear him audibly. These are just a few experiences.

How Do You Put The Word That You Hear Into Action, Into Your Heart?

Take the time to pray about and to answer some or all of the questions and express them in your own creative language.

God's Word

John 1:1-3 says, very clearly, that God is the word, and that through Him everything was made. Everything. You and me. Our ability to talk, write, paint, dance sing, compose, choreograph, sculpt, work with clay, fabricate, weave, carve, engrave, draw. Everything. Everything is made through Him. One has to let this truth seep into one's mind. Everything. The Greek word in the original text is pas (G3956). It means "whoever" and "whatever." It encompasses people, things, actions, possibilities, ways of working, even things that we may not have always associated with creativity.

God also gives us His promise that His word, which He creates, does not return to Him empty (Isa. 55:11). It leaves His mouth, does what He wants it to do, and accomplishes what He sends it to do. He speaks His creation into existence and sends His word into the world. It accomplishes what He wills.

ACTIVATION 14:

SENDING

God can send His word, His statements, and His mind into the world in different ways. Spoken, visually, written, through movement, in all art forms. God made them all. And He saw that it was good.

Does God send His word into the world through your art? Have you ever given or sold art to others? Have you used it during a workshop or prayer? Published online or organised an exhibition? What is God doing with your art in the world? Does He give you new ways to send your art into the world?

Take the time to pray about and to answer some or all of the questions and express them in your own creative language.

Jesus Pronounces Healing

I am happy to give two more examples of how Jesus, the Creator, speaks into existence. In John 4:49, a royal official asked Jesus to rush to his son to heal him. The official was in Cana; the son was lying sick in Capernaum. In the next verse, Jesus answered him and told him to go home as his son was alive. Jesus expressed the fact of the healing, and it happened at the same instant. We should also note that the officer believed the word of Jesus. At Jesus' word, he went home and found his son alive.

The same thing happened in Luke 7:2-10. The centurion of Capernaum sent messengers to Jesus, who was on His way there, and asked Him to heal his sick servant. The centurion also said that Jesus did not have to appear in person, because he believed that all things were under Jesus' authority. Therefore, He would only need to speak one word to heal the servant. In this case, Jesus did not even have to speak the word "healthy"; the healing came while He was boasting about the faith of this non-Jewish centurion. Jesus spoke healing into existence without even saying the word "healing" itself. As a Creator, He knew exactly what this new state was like and sent His word to accomplish what He wanted. Breath-taking, life-giving.

ACTIVATION 15:

LIFE-GIVING WORDS

When did you experience the words of Jesus as breath-taking, as life-giving? Have you ever spent creative time with someone else and seen how your creations affected them and you? Plan to spend such a time together with others and understand it specifically as worship. Watch what happens.

Take the time to pray about and to answer some or all of the questions and express them in your own creative language.

Listen To God's Voice

Elohim certainly does not speak in a human voice. That would make Him much too human-like.

We occasionally hear Him as if someone is talking to us, but that is only part of what He is saying. Scripture interprets His voice in many ways. We are invited to read about what the voice of God sounds like and what it is like.

How does the voice of God sound? The Bible gives us images from nature and images from music to describe it. Psalm 29 is a wonderful source for images from nature that describe God's voice.

The voice of Adonai "is over the waters" (verse 3, CJB); his voice "flashes fiery flames" (verse 7, CJB) and "rocks the desert" (verse 8, CJB).

God's voice is a voice like thunder. It is also like "the roar of rushing waters" (Rev. 14:2, CJB), like thunder that testifies to power (Job 40:9). God puts the primeval flood to flight with His thunderous voice (Ps. 104:7) and answers Jesus' prayer with His own voice in John 12:27-30. The bystanders think it thundered. They stood there like they were struck by thunder.

ACTIVATION 16:

LISTEN!

How often does God speaking have such a powerful effect on you? Do you take His words seriously, or do you push them aside with your feasibility orientation? Do you let God get close to you, do you surrender to Him, or do you shy away from Him?

Take the time to pray about and to answer some or all of the questions and express them in your own creative language.

A Gentle Thunder

The soft murmur with which God speaks to Elijah on the mountain in I Kings 19:12 is demarnah daq qol in the original text. Qol, often translated as murmur or hiss, also means voice of thunder (H6963). So here God's voice is described as a low or gentle thunder. I'm tempted to say, a tamed thunder. Power wrapped in gentleness. Strength covered with mildness. God can also rein in His power to treat us with kindness to gently touch the depths of our soul.

ACTIVATION 17:

BEING STILL

In Psalm 46:10 (AMP), God says:

"Be still and know that I am God."

Are you still enough to feel the gentle touch, to hear that gentle voice? What do you hear, what do you feel when you calm down inside and concentrate completely on God? What is God doing in you, in your creative expression, when you wait so quietly before Him?

Take the time to pray about and to answer some or all of the questions and express them in your own creative language.

An Image From Music

God's voice is described as a trumpet or trombone. In Revelation 4:1 John compares the voice he hears from the open door in heaven to a trumpet. Revelation 1:10 makes it clear that it is Jesus' voice. The word salpigx in Greek, translated as trumpet describes an instrument with a log, straight design that was often played by soldiers (G4536). The same word is used in Hebrews 12:19, which speaks of God's appearance on Mount Sinai, speaking to the people of Israel (Ex. 19:16,19). There, God's voice is described as the sound of shofar horns (rams' horns). At the same time, thunder and lightning as well as flames of fire appear. The shofar was used in war to warn the camp of danger or was blown for gathering. This shows us another link between the Old and New Testaments describing the voice of God.

ACTIVATION 18:

A CRY FOR WAR

The voice of God is described as a war cry. The sound of rams' horns, of trumpets. God calls with His voice to gather us. Is your art a cry for war? Through your artistic expression, have you ever inspired the community to gather? Or have you ever expressed the martial voice of God through creative expression as a group? What would it look like if your art were perceived as the sound of trumpets?

Take the time to pray about and to answer some or all of the questions and express them in your own creative language.

Powerful And Life-Giving

How, then, is the voice of God? It is mighty and glorious (Ps. 29:3-4), but also terrible. Powerful, imposing, influential; brilliant, attractive, amazing, incomparable, exceptional. Psalm 29 is a veritable source of formulation, like a richly laid table. Enjoy the richness of these words.

God's voice gives life. Jesus says in John 5:25 that His voice will give life to those who hear it in the not yet and in the current time. Yes, even the dead will receive life again through His voice. Through God's voice we know to whom we belong, where we are at home, who speaks to us. God's voice gives us favour. This new life contains meaning, joy, and purpose, according to God's will. Such is the voice of God, which He uses to call into existence.

ACTIVATION 19:

AT HOME

God's voice gives life: meaningful, joyful, fulfilled life. When He speaks, you know to whom you belong. Who do you belong to when you paint, write, sing, sculpt, choreograph, dance, or work with fabrics? When God speaks, do you know where your home is? How would you creatively describe this "home," this "belonging"? Be honest with your feelings.

Take the time to pray about and to answer some or all of the questions and express them in your own creative language.

God Sings

God doesn't just use His voice to create from nothing. He also makes other art with it. God the Father and God the Son sing. Does that sound unusual? Have you ever noticed that before? Let's look at the Scriptures. The Father sings about us in Zephaniah 3:17.

"The Lord your God is in your midst, a mighty one who will save; he will rejoice over you with gladness; he will quiet you by his love; he will exult over you with loud singing" (ESV).

"Loud singing" is the translation of the Hebrew rinnah (H7440) and hits the core of its meaning: not only to sing but to sing loudly! God rejoices over you with gladness.

ACTIVATION 20:

REJOICING

God rejoices and exults in you! He sings over you! Do you believe that? Do these statements fit with your idea about yourself? With your own image? Or are they too good to be true? Or do you feel far removed from the image God must have of you when He sings over you?

Why would He not rejoice over you? If you read Zephaniah 3:9-17, you will realise that it is God Himself who causes people to turn to Him! Ask Him to help you turn back to Him when you think He can't sing over you.

Take the time to pray about and to answer some or all of the questions and express them in your own creative language.

God Makes His Songs Heard

The Father also sang about King David. We find this in Psalm 32:7. God surrounds David with songs of deliverance (CJB). The original text makes it quite clear that God is the doer in this verse. The verb in the original text is second person singular, i.e. David says that it is God who surrounds him with these songs, that these songs or shouts (in other translations) come from God. God makes these songs heard, He sings them over David.

ACTIVATION 21:

DELIVERANCE

It can be challenging to see that God surrounds us with songs of deliverance. Have you ever heard them? Have you ever experienced that your art, your picture, your song, your choreography, your sculpture demonstrated the deliverance that comes from God to someone else? This is not a yes/no question; it is a question of degree or intensity. How deep does your art penetrate into what God wants to convey, to show, to hand out? Salvation, deliverance, redemption? Is that expecting too much?

Take the time to pray about and to answer some or all of the questions and express them in your own creative language.

The Son Sings

The New Testament gives us several examples of this. In Hebrews 2:12, the author writes that Jesus, who calls us brothers and sisters, declares to us the name of His father and sings praises to Him in the congregation. This statement is a direct quote from Psalm 22:22, in which it is ostensibly spoken by David. Psalm 22 in its entirety is often called the messianic Psalm of the Cross, since Jesus utters verse one on the cross and a number of other statements of the psalm can be interpreted messianically, such as the abuse in verses six to eight and the description of suffering in verses 12 to 18.

Jesus Sings The Hallel

The second example, in which Jesus also sings in community, occurs in Matthew 26:30 and Mark 14:26. At the end of the Seder meal, which Jesus had reinterpreted as His own death on the cross, Jesus and His disciples sing the Hallell, as the Complete Jewish Bible translates. This would have been Psalms 113 to 118 or excerpts from them. It is quite possible that Jesus and the disciples sang these psalms antiphonally, i.e., Jesus sang the stanzas and the disciples the Hallelujah, the refrain. Again we see the joy that shines forth in God's creation of the world in this song. I would like to pick out four passages from this hymn of praise that Jesus sang after His last Seder meal and call them to your attention.

In Psalm 116:15, it says:

'From ADONAI's point of view, the death of those faithful to him is costly' (CJB).

In Psalm 118:6-7, it says:

"With Adonai on my side, I fear nothing—what can human beings do to me? With Adonai on my side as my help, I will look with triumph at those who hate me" (CJB).

Psalm 118:17 says:

"I will not die, but live,
And tell of the works of the Lord" (NASB).

And finally, Psalm 118:22-23 declares:

"The stone that the builders rejected has become the cornerstone. This is the Lord's doing; it is marvellous in our eyes" (ESV).

How would Jesus have felt when He sang these lines with His disciples, just before the crucifixion, on the way to the Mount of Olives and the Garden of Gethsemane? There are lots of layers. Lots of thoughts that are higher, more complex than ours.

ACTIVATION 22:

COMMUNITY AND DESERT

Jesus sings in community. He is creative in community with His disciples. When was the last time you were creative in community, in the church, with other artists? Did you feel the joy that Jesus expresses through His song of praise as you were creative together? Did you feel something else?

He also sings just before He is arrested. How do you deal with being under pressure, e.g., to produce something or when feeling that you are in a desert, having no inspiration? Do you still praise God? Just try it and see what happens.

Take the time to pray about and to answer some or all of the questions and express them in your own creative language.

God Composes

God is not only the One who sings over us, but He is also a lyricist and composer, another unusual statement. Job says, in 35:10,

"God my Maker, who gives songs in the night" (ESV).

Again, God is the doer in this verse. He gives the songs, they come from Him. They are songs that are accompanied by instruments. The Hebrew word here is zamiyr, the basic meaning of which is "to touch the strings" (H2158). In Psalm 40:3, David writes that God put a new song in his mouth. Again we see the statement that God gives the song, it comes from Him. All things in heaven and on earth were made through Him. God makes His songs available to people.

The New Song

The new song is mentioned in the following scriptures: Psalm 33:3; Psalm 40:3; Psalm 96:1; Psalm 98:1; Psalm 144:9; Psalm 149:1; Isaiah 42:10; Revelation 5:9 and 14:3.

The new song that we may receive from the Lord today is a prophetic song, a rhema word of the Lord

(G4487). It is a specific word or phrase attributed to a specific person or group in a specific situation. It is always alive, effective, and powerful. Of course, it is not received word for word from God on par with the inspiration of Scripture. However, a song from God shares His heart at a specific time in a specific situation.

He indeed gave a prophetic song to a group of intercessors during an intercession and worship time in May 2019, at the highest geographical point of Cyprus. It was a song from Him to us. A group of us had spent time singing, interceding, and prophesying over the nation. This is the spontaneous song we received that morning:

> "I desire your heart,
> I desire your thoughts,
> I want you.
> I desire all spheres of your feelings,
> I desire your mind.
> Come to me as I call.
> Come to me as I call.
> O Bride, surrender everything to me as I call
> upon you."

The new song can also be a singer's song to the Lord. In this case, it is often a hymn of praise (Ps. 149:1). When we sing a new song, we sing what God puts in our mouth. It is Christ in us, the hope of glory (Col. 1:27), singing through us. The Lord Himself arranges what is sung. The river of God's Spirit, His living water, flows out of us in song (John 7:38). We become bearers of His message to individuals, communities, cities, or nations. Being prophetic, the song points to Jesus (Rev. 19:10) and encourages, admonishes and comforts (1 Cor. 14:3). The new song can be sung by an individual or a group in perfect unity. There are lots of layers, lots of meaning to explore in depth.

ACTIVATION 23:

A NEW SONG

The new song is prompted by God Himself. It is His now-word for us. Have you ever received a now-word from God? As a song, as a work of art, vision, sculpture, choreography, or poem? Take time to be quiet before God and listen to Him. What does He say, what does He give you?

> Take the time to pray about and to answer some or all of the questions and express them in your own creative language.

The Song Of God

There is also a song in the Old Testament given by God Himself and written down word for word. In Deuteronomy 31:19, the Lord speaks to Moses. He commands Moses and Joshua to write down a song. The word in the original, kathab, translated as "write down," means to record, not to compose (H3789). That means that the author of the song is clearly God, not Moses. Moses merely records. We find the song in

Deuteronomy 32:1-43. Moses and Joshua recite this song in front of the people. The song speaks of the good things God has done for Israel, Israel's (prophesied) turning away from God, His (future) judgement and His (future) mercy on the people. It is a song that is prophetic.

CHAPTER 3:
GOD COMMUNICATES

God communicates. Clearly. Otherwise, we would not have the Bible. He reveals Himself to us in Scripture. He does this in very different genres. In Scripture, there are historical records, legal texts, lyrical works, prophecies, wisdom texts, eyewitness accounts, and epistles. God communicates artistically in all of these formats.

God Is A Poet

This statement is perhaps not as unusual as some others. He often does not speak in prose form, but in lyrical structures, both in the Old and New Testament. Poetry in Hebrew often does not have the structure that we might be familiar with from English poems. Poetry in Hebrew does not work with rhymes but with rhythms, plays on words, chiasmi, opposites, and parallelisms. In the following sections, I explain the terms "plays on words," "chiasmi" and "parallelisms."

Plays On Words

Here is an example of a play on words. In Jeremiah 1:11-12, God asks Jeremiah what he sees. He replies that he sees the branch of an almond tree. The Lord replies that Jeremiah was right because God watches over His word to carry it out (verse 12, ESV). We don't see any play on words in English here. In the original text, however, God uses a play on words. The Hebrew word for almond tree is shaqed (H8247), the Hebrew word for watch is shoqed (H8245). Since the almond tree is the first tree to bloom in the spring, the play on words means that God's word will be fulfilled first, soon, early.

Activation 24:

Meanings

God knows what He wants to say and how He wants to say it. He plays with meanings, with words, with sentence structures in order to make meanings clear. He plays with different dimensions of language and expresses meaning on several levels. Have you ever played with meanings in your creative expression? Maybe this is something new. What does it look like when you play with different meanings in your painting, in your poem, in your dance, in your sculpture, in your song, in your ceramics, consciously? What is taking place?

Take the time to pray about and to answer some or all of the questions and express them in your own creative language.

Chiasmi

A chiasmus (plural chiasmi) is a rhetorical or literary figure in which words, grammatical structures, or concepts are repeated in reverse order. Very often, the poetic form of the original, biblical text cannot be easily translated into another language.

For those of us who don't speak Hebrew—at least I don't—a chiasmus is harder to understand than a play on words. In a chiasmus, a statement is repeated in reverse order, often around a central statement in the middle of the grammatical construction. This sounds complicated, but it becomes clear when you break down the text into its individual parts. Just read Genesis 1:11 in your Bible. I actually find little poetry in there. Here is a translation in which the reversed statements are made clear:

A Then God said, "Let the earth [erets] sprout vegetation,

B plants yielding seed [zera],

C and fruit [periy] trees on the earth

D bringing forth [asah]

C' fruit [periy] after their kind,

B' with seed [zera] in them;

A' on the earth [erets]." And it was so.

The statements in the original text are in the following chiastic structure: earth, seed, fruit, bringing forth, fruit, seed, earth. "Bringing forth" is then the central statement of the text, as it stands in the middle of the structure! God speaks in poetic form even if it is difficult for us to decipher it in English.

Activation 25:

The Central Statement

What is the central message of your art? Or of a work of art? What is "in the middle"? Is this central statement explained by or set in other elements of your art or your art work? How difficult is it for your "readers" to understand the statement? How do you react when a viewer or spectator experiences or understands a different statement as central? Do you allow this ambiguity? Or do you try to prevent it? Does God have different statements in your work of art that appeal to different viewers or spectators, different statements with which they can connect?

Take the time to pray about and to answer some or all of the questions and express them in your own creative language.

Parallelisms

A parallelism is more likely to be imitated in translations. In Deuteronomy 6:5, God says through Moses that the Israelites are to love God with all their hearts, with all their soul and with all their might (ESV). There are lots of layers, again. Each of these three words has a wide background of meanings that would go beyond the scope of this text if explored in full. But we need to understand the poetry behind them. This phrase is what is called an "emphatic parallelism," a horrible technical term that states that the parallel words reinforce the meaning of the first one. That sounds easier. "Love with all your soul and with all your might" reinforces what is going on in the heart. We may have experienced that before.

We find an example of another parallelism, this time a so-called "emblematic" one, in Isaiah 1:18. In an emblematic parallelism, a statement is supplemented with a metaphor or a comparison. Here, God says to Israel through the prophet that even if their sins be scarlet, yet they will be white as snow; though they are red as crimson, God will wash the Israelites clean as white wool. We can see these parallels in the English translation. Of course, we do not only find this poetic structure in direct statements of God. Such structures run all through the Old Testament and are particularly evident in Psalms and Proverbs.

ACTIVATION 26:

REINFORCEMENTS

How do you reinforce the statements of your art? Or, to put it better: do you reinforce the statements of your art? Do you use comparisons, metaphors, opposites? This works well in writing and in dancing. Try painting or sculpting. Try it out with colours and textures.

Take the time to pray about and to answer some or all of the questions and express them in your own creative language.

Jesus as a Poet

Although the New Testament was written in Greek, we have good reason to believe that Jesus spoke Hebrew (the language of the learned) and Aramaic (which Josephus the historian described as "the language of our land"). We can assume that Jesus' thinking was shaped by Hebrew or related Aramaic structures, not by Greek ones. This is actually logical when you look at His ancestry, the circumstances of His birth, and His culture. It is therefore not surprising that we find, for example, both playing with opposites and parallelisms, as were common in Hebrew and Aramaic, in Jesus' communication.

Playing with opposites is found in many statements

about the kingdom of God, which is an "upside-down" kingdom. We find a good description of this contrast, related to the power structures of the world in Matthew 23:11. Jesus says that the greatest among them should be the servant of all. We have to turn our usual thinking upside down in order to understand and practice this. The Beatitudes are a prime example of playing with opposites. In Matthew 5:3-11 we find the following contrasts in the NASB:

The poor in spirit will possess the kingdom of heaven.

Those who mourn shall be comforted.

The gentle shall inherit the earth, i.e. become mighty.

Those who hunger and thirst for righteousness will be satisfied.

Jesus speaks in the poetic structure in which He grew up, speaking Hebrew and probably also Aramaic. Jesus has been called the "invisible poet" in literature.

ACTIVATION 27:

HEADSTAND

Is your art part of the upside down kingdom? Or does your art fit seamlessly into the prevailing creative structures of "that's how it works today"? To what extent does your art turn existing structures, frameworks, and sensitivities, which one may silently or thoughtlessly accept as given, upside down? Is that not what you intend to do? What does God intend with your art? That is an open-ended question that involves a lot of headstands. Might you offend someone when you express certain things creatively?

Take the time to pray about and to answer some or all of the questions and express them in your own creative language.

Parallelisms In The Words Of Jesus

The statements of Jesus overflow with parallelisms. In Luke 6:37-38, we see an emphatic, reinforcing parallelism. Jesus tells His disciples and a great multitude of people that if they give, they will be given: a good, pressed down, shaken together, and running-over measure (NASB). Four parallel, if not synonymous, expressions that embellish the first statement.

Antithetical parallelisms work with opposites. In Luke 6:27-28, Jesus skilfully clothes His statements in such a matrix:

> "Love your enemies, do good to those who hate you, bless those who curse you, pray for those who are abusive to you" (NASB).

It is another creative paraphrase of the upside-down kingdom. In Matthew 10:39, Jesus says:

> "The one who has found his life will lose it, and the one who has lost his life on My account will find it" (NASB).

In Matthew 23:12 he takes the same line:

> "Whoever exalts himself shall be humbled, and whoever humbles himself shall be exalted" (NASB).

It is a poetic statement, working with counterpoints, formulated by the Creator Himself. It is a statement we as artists should take seriously.

ACTIVATION 28:

COUNTERPOINTS

Taking something seriously. Counterpoints that God uses to make His statements clear. Where does God set counterparts in your art, in your works? Is your art a voice against the standards of this world, to which we are not supposed to conform (Rom 12:2)? Is this question pleasant or unpleasant? Perhaps take more time than usual to answer these questions.

Take the time to pray about and to answer some or all of the questions and express them in your own creative language.

Jesus, An "Activational" Speaker

Jesus is more than a motivational speaker. More than one who appeals to our feelings. He gives peoples tools to help them change the framework, the matrix through which they see and understand the world. In this respect, I like to call Him an "activational" speaker, one who activates us to act. Activated to change. Be doers of the word. When we allow ourselves to be transformed by Jesus' statements, which He articulates so skilfully that they touch our hearts and not just our brains, change flows into action. It accelerates the more deeply we allow ourselves to be changed, like a river tumbling down a mountain into the sea. Full steam ahead!

ACTIVATION 29:

ADDRESSING THE HEART

Jesus gives us tools to change our matrix and the matrix of others. What instruments do you have in your hands? Or in your feet? In your body?

Has Jesus already changed you through your art, the action flowing from His speech? Has He already changed others through your art, the action flowing from His speech? Is this claim too high? Should we face this claim?

Do Jesus' words not only hit you in the head, but also in the heart? Does your art not only hit the viewer or spectator in the head, but also in the heart?

Take the time to pray about and to answer some or all of the questions and express them in your own creative language.

Jesus speaks a lot in parables, a metaphorical discourse that describes a condition while inviting change. Much has been written about Jesus' parables. So I won't bore anyone with a rehash of what has already been released. It is important, however, to understand here, that Jesus speaking in parables shows us that He is a word artist, one who consciously uses words and language to invite us to change the conditions that occurred after the fall. And arguably, He is the best one who ever lived. Irresistible.

Let us also pay attention to the way Jesus teaches when He does not speak in parables. For the most part, He does not teach like a preacher today. I can only find two passages in the New Testament that I could see as Jesus' sermons: the Sermon on the Mount (Matt. 5-7) and the Discourse on the Mount of Olives (Matt. 24-25).

Jesus is often called a teacher, as in Matthew 19:16. Here the rich young ruler asks Him what (good) he must do to gain eternal life. Some English translation here use "master," not "teacher." When the Pharisees and later the Sadducees want to lure Jesus into a trap, they also address Him as a teacher (Matt. 22:16 and 24. NASB).

In doing so, they at least admit that He is addressed this way across the board. He teaches with authority. At the end of the Sermon on the Mount, His listeners were deeply impressed. He teaches with authority, not like the scribes (Matt. 7:28, NASB).

Activation 30:

Authority

Jesus taught with authority. The original word is exousia (G1849). It occurs over a hundred times in the New Testament and has a wide range of meanings: power, capability, competence, freedom, ability, influence, energy, strength, even guts. Take a little more time and go through each of these meanings with the question of whether and how you have, use, practice and manifest these qualities in your art. Yes? No? Some more, maybe? Others not? Which? With which of these attributes do you invite the viewer, the observer or the participant in your art to change?

Take the time to pray about and to answer some or all of the questions and express them in your own creative language.

Jesus, The Walking Teacher

Jesus is often shown in the New Testament to be a teacher who travels around. He goes from place to place with His disciples and talks to them. In John 4, Jesus goes from Judea through Samaria to Galilee with His disciples. He uses the opportunity during a rest stop to start a conversation with a Samaritan, the woman at the well. In John 4:1-43, we read the entire encounter. Through Jesus' prophetic speaking, the whole village came to believe in Him. I find it remarkable that Genesis 3:8-9 also shows us God walking in the Garden wanting to meet Adam and Eve, desiring to encounter them. It is one of the Father's methods that Jesus continued and uses artfully to teach His disciples and others. Father and Son pull together here. When Jesus calls His first disciples, He says, "Follow me."

It is a call to leave everything behind and walk with Him. He will go with them and teach them. This spoken-word artist uses movement to bring clarity to thoughts. Modern brain researchers explain to us that the rhythm of walking promotes the transmission of thoughts from short-term to long-term memory.

CHAPTER 4: GOD CULTIVATES THE GARDEN

God as a gardener? Now, that's an idea. Maybe with a slouch hat and a shovel? Yes, such representations actually exist. In John 20:15, Mary turns to Jesus, whom she has not yet recognised, at the open tomb. She thinks that He is the gardener. The word in the original text is kepouros, which can also mean something like a guardian, keeper, or caretaker (G2780).

A Unique Word

This word is only used in this one place in the New Testament, nowhere else. In verse 17, Jesus tells Mary not to touch Him. The Latin translation of this statement, noli me tangere, is a theme in Christian art, particularly from the 14th to the 18th centuries. An online search of this Latin statement yields a multitude of images showing Jesus as a gardener. Even with a floppy hat.

In several places in Scripture, however, God is directly or indirectly referred to as a gardener. In Isaiah 60:21, God says that Israel will possess the land as a branch of His planting (NASB). He is saying that He Himself is planting the land, and He makes a similar statement in Ezekiel 34:29. Here, too, He speaks of the fact that He does the planting Himself.

ACTIVATION 31:

GOD CULTIVATES US

How do you experience God as a guardian, keeper, or caretaker? Is that who He is for you? What would have to happen so that you would see God more as a caretaker in your artistic work or see that He is looking after you? Where and how are you planted? Do you believe that God planted you where you are today? How would you describe this position, these circumstances, your creative status quo?

Take the time to pray about and to answer some or all of the questions and express them in your own creative language.

Being Creative As A Gardener

As a gardener, how does God watch, guard, and care for us? I asked friends of mine who are full-time gardeners. Suzi Irwin wrote that the most obvious thing is the design, the planning, God as a designer. She sees planning a garden like conducting an orchestra. Just as different instruments take over the main part in different phases of a piece of music, different plants come to the fore in different seasons. The Creator planned this really well. There are endless ways to combine textures, colours and shapes, like a 3-D painting. God's ways are unlimited. The design of a garden includes the opportunity to create a space for peace and tranquillity in the busyness of life. Doesn't that sound like the Garden of Eden? God gives us peace and rest. Seeds and bulbs give us hope for the future. God is our hope.

Paul Graham, another friend, wrote that a garden helps us see and appreciate space, colour, movement and form. God plays with these elements in creation. We see His playful joy, His will. The design of a garden can invite us on a visual journey and provide a direction of movement. A garden can hold surprises, hide things, and create intimacy, an intimacy that God sought with man in Genesis 3:8-9.

ACTIVATION 32:

THE DESIGNER

Do you experience God as a designer in your own life? In your artistic expression? Do you see different phases in your artistic development? Do you see that there are still a lot of phases and stages in the development of your art.

Are you experiencing the journey, the intimate journey that God has embarked upon with you in your art, the journey that He wants to continue to embark on?

Do you experience calm and peace in your creative process or in the creation of a work? Do you see God's design in your works? Do you value what God puts in your hands and feet?

> Take the time to pray about and to answer some or all of the questions and express them in your own creative language.

The Grapevine And The Vinedresser

In John 15, Jesus describes Himself as the true vine and His Father as the vinedresser, the one who watches, guards, and cares. The vinedresser takes away the branches that bear no fruit and cleanses the branches that bear fruit so that they may multiply their fruit even more (verse 2). The secret of the branch bearing much fruit is that it remains on the vine (verse 4). That is, if we abide in Jesus, He abides in us (same verse) and we bear much fruit (verse 5).

ACTIVATION 33:

THE VINEDRESSER

What would you describe as the fruit of your artistic work? Do you find this question difficult? Look at how you can stay on the vine and notice what juice, what elixir of life flows from the vine into your fruit. Do you always devote yourself to the vinedresser protecting, tending, and caring for you, or are you sometime an unwilling, unruly branch? A branch that does not understand or does not see its development or how this development fits together with its previous ideas and insights?

> Take the time to pray about and to answer some or all of the questions and express them in your own creative language.

Eden And Gethsemane

Two gardens are of particular importance in Scripture. In the Garden of Eden, the decision that brought mankind down was made; in the Garden of Gethsemane, the decision that brought people back into relationship with the Father was made. Adam and Eve chose to eat from the tree, which God said not to eat (Gen. 3:3). Eden gives us a first glimpse of a sacred place of encounter between God and man. A place of harmony. Today this place of encounter is our own body, the temple of the Holy Spirit (1 Cor. 6:19), in which God now watches, guards and cares (Col.1:27). God Himself plants this garden in Eden (Gen. 2:8). He meets Adam and Eve there in the cool of the evening (Gen. 3:8).

Gethsemane, at the foot of the Mount of Olives, is the garden in the New Testament where Jesus makes the decision to walk the path to the cross to the end (Matt. 26:39, 42 and 44). I find it remarkable that as Jesus comes to the end of this path confirmed in the garden, He tells one of the criminals next to Him on a cross that he will be with Him in paradise on the same day. The Greek word paradeisos comes from a root meaning park, garden, or plantation (G3857). They met the gardener the same day.

ACTIVATION 34:

A PLACE OF ENCOUNTER

A place of encounter between man and God. Even the cross was a place of encounter between man and God. How do you meet the gardener? In the harmony of Eden, in the intensity of the cross? In your own body, the temple of the Holy Spirit? In your own creativity? Open, locked, honest, bashful, trusting?

Take the time to pray about and to answer some or all of the questions and express them in your own creative language.

The Garden As A Symbol

It is important to understand what gardens symbolise in Scripture in order to better understand what the description of God as a gardener means. Gardens in the Old Testament represent security and stability. They are untouchable protected areas and indicate being sheltered. This is what God the gardener gives us. The garden was an established metaphor.

Let us look at the Song of Songs. In 4:12, we see a locked garden:

> "A locked garden is my sister, my bride, a locked spring, a sealed fountain" (NASB).

The sealed garden signifies purity and piety, reserved for a worthy purpose and defended. At Jewish weddings, there was an equivalent prayer: "Let no stranger enter the sealed well."

We see the opposite in 5:1:

> "I have come into my garden, my sister, my bride; I have gathered my myrrh along with my balsam. I have eaten my honeycomb with my honey; I have drunk my wine with my milk" (NASB).

Now the garden is open. It is described in emphatic, reinforcing parallelisms. There is the lyrical form again. The bride now opens up to her groom. There are rich hints in the parallelisms. Intimacy that is protected and defended. We see what God gives us, what He artfully plans, when He is called the gardener.

ACTIVATION 35:

BEING SHELTERED

God as a gardener stands for stability, security, being sheltered, and intimacy. We see this in the Song of Songs. Are you safe in God during your creative process? Are you looking to Him or only to yourself with what you do in your creative process? Do you feel secure in your creative actions? What does it mean for you to be "sheltered"? Do you encounter God in your art in an intimate, personal, familiar way? When and how?

> Take the time to pray about and to answer some or all of the questions and express them in your own creative language.

God Brings Forth And Releases

This becomes clear in Isaiah 61:11. Here God Himself is compared to the garden. The garden (God) produces plants (His disciples) from seed just as the earth produces plants. Let us not lose sight of the fact that the verbs are used causatively in both parts of the verse. "Causes to spring up" shows us that the earth is the initiator of the growth of the crops, just as God is the initiator of the sprout from the seed. In the original text, the causality is expressed in the grammatical form of the verb.

We find these metaphors elsewhere in Scripture as well. In Psalm 80: 9-10, Asaph describes Israel as a vine that God brought out of Egypt and planted in a new land. God is seen here implicitly as a vinedresser and planter. We see causality again, as we did in Isaiah 61:11. In Hosea 10:1, Israel is reminded that it is a vine that should prosper.

This metaphor is continued in the New Testament. In John 15:1-5, Jesus describes Himself as the true vine and His Father as the vinedresser. In verse 5, Jesus says He is the vine and we disciples are the branches. Whoever abides in Him and He in them bears much fruit. Apart from Him, we can do nothing. This means that the care, watch, and protection that God as the gardener bestows on the vine flows into the branches. We benefit, we feed off the art with which God as a gardener tends the vine and thus us as branches. Remain in me, and I will remain in you.

A golden vine stood over the entrance to the Holy Place in the Second Temple. If someone brought gold in the form of a vine leaf, a single grape, or a whole bunch of grapes as a voluntary offering, the priests would hang it on the vine. We can see that Jesus may also be drawing a parallel to the entrance of the Holy Place in the temple when He calls Himself the "true vine."

ACTIVATION 36:

IN HIS KINGDOM

God brings forth. His actions are causative, He is the cause of your art, your motive. Is that so? Does He move you toward your artistic expression? This is a slightly different aspect than before. How is God the source, the very essence of your works? Did He bring you forth as an artist, did He call you into life and form you as an artist? Did He free you in your creative work and created a broad space for you, so that you can conquer the entire land given to you? Is it like Asaph says in Psalm 80? Can you see this space, this sphere of influence, this territory? Are you already in it? Did you conquer it? Where is the horizon?

> Take the time to pray about and to answer some or all of the questions and express them in your own creative language.

Sower And Lord Of The Harvest

Two other metaphors for God that are similar to the gardener are the sower and the Lord of the harvest. In the parable of the sower (Luke 8:4-8), the planter goes out and sows seed. It falls on four different grounds. The seed beside the road will be trampled on and eaten by the birds; the seed on rocky soil withers; the seed amongst the thorns gets choked out. The last ground is the high-yielding one, in which the seed bears fruit up to a hundredfold. Jesus explains to His disciples that the seed is the word of God. The word comes first from God (2 Tim. 3:16-17) and bears fruit (Isa. 55:11). The sower is a metaphor for God, the One who gives and distributes the word.

At the same time, He is Lord of the harvest. In Matthew 13:27 in the parable of the tares among the wheat, the landowner on whose field the seed was sown, makes the decisions. Since this is a parable about the kingdom of heaven, here again the one who owns the field and thus the harvest is a metaphor for God.

He separates the wheat from the chaff (Matt. 3:12) with His shovel and sends workers into the harvest (Matt. 9:38). We need them more than ever.

ACTIVATION 37:

SOWING AND HARVESTING

God is the One who sows. What type of soil are you? How can you refine and develop the texture, the quality of your soil? Where would you need to invest? Quality has its price. Is there a price you are willing to pay to develop your soil? Is there a quantum leap that you have been planning for a long time? A leap of faith? Do you dare?

God is also the Lord of the harvest. Whatever He does with or through your art belongs to Him. He is the Lord. Is that difficult sometimes? Or is it sometimes difficult to see what He is doing with and through your art in others or even yourself? Do you let yourself be sent by the Lord of the harvest or do you make the decisions yourself?

> Take the time to pray about and to answer some or all of the questions and express them in your own creative language.

We Are Planted

What does the gardener who tills the field, cultivates the vine and sends out workers do with us? He plants us by streams of water (Ps. 1:3), i.e. He provides us with what we need in order to thrive so that we can put down good, deep, strong roots that can support a big tree. Lots of fruit.

God also calls us trees of righteousness, a planting of the Lord for His glory (Isa. 61:3). "Planting" is the original Hebrew matta, which can also be translated as "vineyard" or "garden" (H4302). It is a vineyard or garden cultivated by the gardener for His glory. We are trees of righteousness, not to be praised ourselves, but for others. And first for the Lord. The work of His hands, to His glory. A Hebrew proverb says, "Like the gardener, so the garden."

CHAPTER 5:

GOD FORMS US LIKE CLAY

The potter is a symbolism for God used in the Old and New Testament. Isaiah 64:8 states the central statement on this subject:

"But now, LORD, you are our Father; We are the clay and You our potter, and all of us are the work of Your hand."

The Potter Works On Clay

We are the clay. The word in the original text is chomer. It originally meant "something that bubbles up" and was used to describe clay (H2563). Clay is a pile of loam that has been cleaned. Air bubbles erupt from it. Clay is not my form of preferred creative expression. That is why I asked potters to explain to me how pottery works. First the potter cuts a piece of clay from the block and beats it to release the air bubbles that are in the clay and will affect its integrity. Beating the clay can be compared to kneading bread dough, but it takes more force because the clay has a denser consistency. With bread dough, however, air is more likely to be kneaded in; with clay it has to be expelled.

During my research to this approach, I asked myself what it is that is bubbling up in me and what God has already thrown out to improve my steadfastness.

ACTIVATION 38:

BUBBLING UP

In Isaiah 64:8, the prophet mentions the potter and the Father as metaphors for God in one breath. This already shows us that the potter's work on us will be done with intimate love. Do you find it loving when God works on you like clay? When God is drumming the bubbles out of you, what bubbles up? What is it that you let go of to let Him transform you into a better, more mature, stronger, more intense, more purposeful instrument of His actions?

Are you willing or unwilling? Perhaps it is time to look deeper into our own motivations and see what may still need to bubble up and be eliminated so that we are refined like silver (Zec. 13:9)?

> Take the time to pray about and to answer some or all of the questions and express them in your own creative language.

Moulding

When all the air has been worked out of the clay, it can be moulded by hand or with tools. It is often formed on a potter's wheel. The advantage here is that it can be centred on the disk so that the shape does not become crooked or one-sided. The potter has to use some force to keep the clay in the centre of the wheel as it has a life of its own and tries to fly off the wheel. We, too, often have a life of our own, trying to escape the dynamics with which God is working on us. Once the clay is properly centred, it stays in the middle of the disc. It is good that God works on us with an appropriate degree of pressure, so that we don't become one-sided or keep biased views.

When the clay is centred, the potter presses his fingers into the clay to open up the middle and begins to shape the outlines with his hands. The potter makes even and calm movements. Correct positioning of the fingers gives shape; constant calm and clear guidance achieves the best results.

When the basic shape is in place, the potter begins to expand the form. This is often a growth process for us. Meanwhile, the potter is in continuous contact with the clay, touching it constantly. In doing so, God once again takes us out of our comfort zone and gives us things to do that we do not yet seem to be equipped for or empowered to do. God does not choose the talented, He equips the chosen.

In this process, we might come into conflict with the potter. What if we don't like the shape or the purpose? Should the clay put itself on a par with the potter or believe that the potter does not know what he is doing (Isa. 29:16)?

Then the clay would be reminded that it is a piece of pottery among the pieces of the earth (Isa. 45:9).

The potter is the one who makes the decision as to the shape and purpose of the vessel, determining which way it is right in the eyes of the potter (Jer. 18:4). The potter has power over the clay to make a vessel of honour or of common use (Rom. 9:21). As the clay fits into the master's hands, so we find our way into God's plans. After all, we are clay vessels in which the bright light of the Gospel shines, the treasure given to us (2 Cor. 4:7).

ACTIVATION 39:

LET YOURSELF BE MOULDED

How does it feel to be on the potter's wheel? Do you sometimes get a little dizzy while God centres you, is being intensely devoted to you? God's attention is on you in these processes so that you don't become crooked or skewed, so that nobody can put you in a bad light.

As God forms you, He is in constant contact with you, constantly in direct touch. He gives you clear guidance. Do you have experience with this? How does it feel? Do you shy away from it, or do you run towards it with open arms?

You can also ask yourself the same questions as you reflect on your growth process as an artist, when God begins to expand the vessel. This process can also be challenging or painful, He touches you and does not always let you see the end from the beginning. How are you doing in these processes?

> Take the time to pray about and to answer some or all of the questions and express them in your own creative language.

Fire And Glaze

When the raw form is ready, it needs to dry slowly for the right amount of time. This is a period of waiting and preparation when we can easily become impatient. The pot must be completely free of moisture before it goes into the first firing, known as the 'bisque' firing, at 1000 degrees Centigrade. Now most of the imperfections are burned out of the vessel. After this firing, the form is hard but still porous. Next it needs to be glazed. Glazing serves to make earthenware impermeable to water. That is, it prevents the intrusion of new disruptive factors. Now the potter will also make soft and gentle changes that will bring out the beauty of the vessel and reflect the potter's creativity and sense of beauty.

To seal the glaze, the vessel is then placed in another fire, reaching temperatures up to 1200 degrees Centigrade. So, don't be surprised if you thought you survived the fire, and there is a second, even hotter round to come. During this firing, the glaze forms a thin layer of glass on the surface, which later reflects the surrounding light. Now nothing can penetrate the vessel and it can be used for its intended purpose.

ACTIVATION 40:

PERIODS OF WAITING

Waiting and preparation, especially in recurring phases, is often challenging. How do you deal with such waiting times? Especially if you cannot yet fathom the purpose of waiting? What does active waiting look like to you?

And how do you feel in the fire? How much strength and freedom from disruptive factors have you already developed? How much décor is there on the vessel that reflects the creativity and beauty of the potter? How much of the light of the ultimate artist is reflected off you? Is there anything you need to do?

> Take the time to pray about and to answer some or all of the questions and express them in your own creative language.

Shaped To Be Beautiful

A priest once visited an artist's house. There he saw an extraordinarily beautiful vase of flowers standing on the table. Impressed by its elegance, he asked: "Can I buy this vase?" "No," said the artist. The priest tried to persuade him and kept increasing his offer. The potter finally said: "Even for all the riches of the world I will not sell this vase to anyone." The priest was dumbfounded and asked: "What is so special about this flower vase?"

The artist replied, "I lived in gambling, alcohol, fraudulent labour and even vandalism for many years. But one day I went to a church and was deeply touched by a sermon: God can change our lives if we give ourselves into His hands. I was deeply inspired. When I went home, I found a pile of clay by the roadside. I stopped, took a lump of clay home, and made this vase. Every day I looked at this vase and thought about how a lump of clay could be shaped into something so beautiful. I then thought of myself and gave myself to God. Since then, my life has changed completely. I turned from my evil ways and began to experience new life, more joy, peace, and comfort. I made new friends and my business started to prosper."

We are the clay. God formed Adam from the dust of the earth. Adam and earth (adamah) are a play on words in Hebrew. "Dust of the earth" is the Hebrew aphar min adamah. Unlike chomer, aphar does not focus on something that bubbles up, but rather on the consistency of the dust (H6083)—like a powder that first has to be mixed with water.

"Shaped" is the Hebrew yatsar, which also means to press something into a mould, to work as a potter, and to determine a shape (H3335). God formed Adam from clay, working like a potter.

CHAPTER 6:

GOD PLANS AND BUILDS

The Old and New Testaments show us that God builds. Solomon says something very fundamental about this is Psalm 127:1:

"Unless the Lord builds the house,
They who build it labour in vain" (NASB).

We see that God builds houses. That is, He also gives construction plans that come directly from Him. God promises David in 1 Chronicles 17:10 that He will build him a house, not the other way around! Remarkable. The blueprint for this house, which is more likely to be the kingdom or dynasty of David than a house of stone, is from God. I think I have overlooked that many times.

God not only says that He builds, but also that He will build again. In Psalm 102:16, we find His promise to rebuild Zion; in Psalm 147:2, His promise applies to Jerusalem. In Jeremiah 24:6, God makes the same promise but makes His character clear through two metaphors: He will build Israel up and not overthrow them and He will plant them and not uproot them. This is also a nice example of a parallelism that works with opposites. God is a poet, gardener, and builder. What a great God. He also promises to rebuild the fallen Tabernacle of David (Amos 9:11, AMP). Much has been written about when and how this will come to pass. This promise was so important and so present to the Jews that it was quoted at the Apostles' meeting in Jerusalem in the course of the evangelisation of the gentiles (Acts 15:16). It is important for us to understand that it is God who is rebuilding here, not man.

ACTIVATION 41:

WHO IS ACTING?

Is God the active one in your life? Or is it you? What is God building with you? Is it a hut, a country estate, a villa, a home, a hermitage according to His plans? What do you think? Do you know the blueprints, the designs for what God wants to do in your life? What is He going to do with you? What questions would you like to ask Him?

> Take the time to pray about and to answer some or all of the questions and express them in your own creative language.

Jesus The Architect

God not only builds, He Himself also gives us the

architect's plans and the artistic designs for the things He envisions. He gives the plans for the ark (Gen. 6:14-17), and Noah carries them out. He gives the plans for the tabernacle, its furniture and furnishings (Ex. 36), and Bezalel, Oholiab, and the other artisans, to whom the Lord has given wisdom and understanding for the building of the sanctuary, carry them out. He gives the plans for the garments of the high priest (Ex. 39:1-31): Bezalel, Oholiab, and the other artists weave them. He gives the building plans for the temple (1 Chr. 28:11-12), which the ministry groups of the priests and Levites and experienced workers carry out. Even Solomon's ally, King Hiram of Tyre, sends builders and materials to carry out God's plans. We see God as a multifaceted designer: as a constructor, furniture designer, and a couturier.

His nature as an architect and master builder is also made clear in two of Jesus' parables. First in the parable of the vineyard owners and the vine-growers in Mark 12:1-12. Here, God is the One who plans (designs and builds) the vineyard, fences it (gives protection), sets up a winepress (makes it work), and builds a watchtower (adds a security system). In the parable, the analogy between the owner of the vineyard and God reaches so far that the vine-growers eventually kill the owner's son and throw him out of the vineyard. Jesus prophesied what the chief priests, the scribes, and the leaders of the people would do to Him. Secondly in the parable of the labourers in the vineyard in Matthew 20:1-16, which deals with the fact that God's love is the same for everyone, God is compared to the owner of the vineyard, who pays the same wages at the end of the day to all labourers.

ACTIVATION 42:

THE BUILDER

Do you recognize God as a diverse Creator who gives you artistic designs in your respective creative expression? Have you seen God arm you with wisdom and understanding to bring about the things He has in mind?

How do you understand the idea that we are only labourers, pilgrims, and transients with a home in heaven (Phil. 3:20), who will give an account? What influence does this knowledge have on your creative processes?

> Take the time to pray about and to answer some or all of the questions and express them in your own creative language.

Jesus The Builder

The builder is the one who is responsible for the construction, who knows how to do it and sees to it that the job is done neatly. Jesus is the builder of His church. He tells Peter that He, Jesus Himself, will build His church. It will be so impenetrable that even the power of death will not be able to defeat her (Matt. 16:18). Protected, secure and resilient, therefore powerful and resistant. Jesus is the cornerstone that supports the building and holds it together. Through Him, the components are firmly connected to each other and grow into a temple in the Lord (Eph. 2:20-21). Jesus builds each one of us up as a living stone in His spiritual house (1 Pet. 2:5).

ACTIVATION 43:

LIVING STONES

To what extent are you protected, secure, resilient, efficient, and resistant? Do you welcome this interpretation of Jesus' statement that His church will be so impenetrable that even the power of death cannot overcome it? Are you part of the church of which Jesus is the head, and do you experience the support, fellowship, devotion, and unity that leads to the invincibility of the disciples?

Do you let yourself be used in this building process? Are you a living or a dead stone? Paralysed with fear of doing something wrong, or active, secure, reconciled, and energetic? What are the reasons for this?

Take the time to pray about and to answer some or all of the questions and express them in your own creative language.

Building The New Temple

It is also Jesus who rebuilds the temple. In John 2:19, He said that in three days He would rebuild the temple after it was torn down. However, He did not mean the physical temple but His own resurrection on the third day after His crucifixion, the rebuilding of the temple of His own body, i.e., the church that would become His own body (Rom. 12:4-6). This restoration of the temple is already foretold in Zechariah 6:12:

"Behold, there is a Man whose name is Branch, for He will branch out from where He is; and He will build the temple of the Lord" (NASB).

Today we as the church of Christ are God's building (1 Cor. 3:9). Today we are the temple of the Holy Spirit, the meeting place between God and us (1 Cor. 3:16). Today we are the house of prayer and devotion (Isa. 56:7). Jesus has us under construction, not with lifeless stones but with living ones. It is He who has the plan and knows how to do it.

CHAPTER 7:

JESUS IS A CREATIVE

Working with your hands.

What is a tekton?

Twice in the New Testament, Jesus is addressed as the son of a craftsman (Matt. 13:55).

There is wide debate as to how to translate this term correctly. Suggested translations include carpenter, builder, architect, metal worker, or craftsman. Carpenter is probably the best-known translation. Jesus clearly had a manual, i.e. artistic profession. The term tekton in Greek often also includes the idea that the person teaches or trains people! Interpretations of this term and the background from which Jesus came range from a poor background, the son of a humble carpenter, to a middle-class background and the assumption that Joseph was an architect. This would imply Joseph was running a workshop with apprentices or associates. At this point I would like to refer to Luke 2:24; Luke reports that Joseph and Mary came to the temple to consecrate Jesus to the Lord and to give the cleansing sacrifice according to what has been stated in the Law of the Lord:

"A PAIR OF TURTLEDOVES OR TWO YOUNG PIGEONS" (NASB).

The quote from the law refers to Leviticus 12:8. There it is decreed that the woman who gives the cleansing sacrifice sacrifices these doves, "if she cannot afford a lamb" (NASB).

That is, if she is poor. Luke that states that Jesus' parents did not have the means for a lamb, i.e., they did not belong to the middle or upper class of their people, at least at the time of His birth.

Herod Antipas, son of Herod the Great, ruler of Galilee and Perea, rebuilt Sepphoris, the capital of the province of Judea between AD 16 and 19. The city was later referred to as the "Ornament of Galilee." Sepphoris was five kilometres northwest of Nazareth. One can well imagine that Joseph and his apprentice son were involved in this construction project close to home, perhaps not as an architect with a workshop but as skilled builders.

I can well imagine that Jesus was a skilled carpenter. He was someone who worked with His hands. As a carpenter He must have known how to make a yoke.

This is an image He used in Matthew 11:28-30. He will also have known how to build a plough. This is an image He used in Luke 9:62. Even in the Old Testament, it says that God works with His hands: In Psalm 143:5, David addresses God directly and says that He speaks of the works of His (God's) hands.

ACTIVATION 44:

THE MASTERPIECE

The Son of God, who calls you back into the healed relationship with God, His Father, had an artistic, craft profession. He worked with His hands. This shows you that as an artist working with your hands (and feet), you are firmly grounded in the earthly life lived by God's son. What does that tell you about your position in the church? Do you belong? Are you outside? Are you only tolerated? Or are you a Living Stone?

You are the work of His hands (Eph. 2:10). Do you feel this way? Are you God's masterpiece? If yes, why? If not, why not?

> Take the time to pray about and to answer some or all of the questions and express them in your own creative language

Working Artistically

What is a charash?

A look at the Old Testament, in which craftsmen are described in detail, also helps us to clarify these terms. Following the wisdom of the translators of the Septuagint, the oldest surviving Greek translation of the Old Testament, the Old Testament equivalent of tekton is the Hebrew charash (H2796). This term includes someone who works with any material, a craftsman, carpenter, engraver, mason, or blacksmith. Only if this word is supplemented in the Old Testament can one identify the specific craftsman.

The term charash ets describes a craftsman in wood, i.e., a carpenter or joiner. In the Septuagint this phrase is translated tekton xylon. We see this in 2 Kings 12:11, 2 Samuel 5:11, or Isaiah 44:13. In reverse conclusion, one could formulate that tekton does not describe a specific profession like a carpenter in the New Testament without a supplementary description but merely states that the person who works in this way earned his money with his hands. There are lots of layers, lots of meaning open to interpretation.

ACTIVATION 45:

ASSIGNING VALUE

Tekton seems to include a range of crafts. Likewise, charash. All these crafts can be included, can be manifested in the work of Jesus' hands. This also means that none of these crafts is better or worse. Has anyone ever told you that your specific creative expression has less value or importance than another? It has happened to me before. Various expressions, however, are worth the same thing.

But how do you determine the value of a creative process or work? Do you value something according to how accustomed you are to it? According to if it is being used in the service of your church or not? Are there creative processes that you miss being practiced in your church, community or group? Processes that are neither seen nor valued?

> Take the time to pray about and to answer some or all of the questions and express them in your own creative language.

A Craftsman With Wisdom And Power?

Not everyone finds it easy to understand that Jesus had a manual trade and at the same time was a master teacher who walked with His disciples for three years. Besides the fact that He is God's son and saves us, of course. He was someone who not only taught but also worked miracles. But the people in His home village reacted with a lack of understanding when they exclaimed:

"Is this not the carpenter's son? Is His mother not called Mary, and His brothers, James, Joseph, Simon, and Judas? And His sisters, are they not all with us?

Where then did this man acquire all these things?" (Matt. 13:55-56, NASB).

But the craftsman's son already had such considerable know-how at the age of twelve that the scribes in the temple and His parents were amazed at His understanding and His answers (Luke 2:47-48). Four verses later it says that Jesus grew and His wisdom continued to increase! We see the same things in Matthew 7:29. After the Sermon on the Mount, the audience is deeply impressed. Jesus taught with authority given to Him by God—unlike their scribes. This was clear to them even if the people in His home town didn't want to accept it.

ACTIVATION 46:

CALLED AS AN ARTIST

Do you accept what Jesus is telling you? Do you see the power and strength in Jesus' statements? What is He saying about your art and your creative processes? Do you believe what He says? Do you believe that Jesus called you as an artist and that He is making an impact through your art? Do you believe that His authority and wisdom are being expressed in your art? How?

Take the time to pray about and to answer some or all of the questions and express them in your own creative language.

CHAPTER 8:

A GOD WHO DANCES?

Jumping For Joy: Giyl

God the Father rejoices over us with joy (Zeph. 3:17). The word rendered in English 'rejoice' has a meaning that describes physical movement. The Hebrew giyl literally means "to whirl about under the influence of intense emotion" (H1523). That sounds more like ecstasy. Rejoicing communicates a verbal expression rather than a physical movement. If you tame this movement or sweep it under a rug, then the result is something you cannot understand as dancing any more. But if you see God in your mind's eye, whirling about us in intense emotion, in exuberant joy, then you understand more easily that you can see God also as a dancer. Is this too farfetched?

God the son is in a similar motion. Let us look at Luke 10:21. The English translation says that Jesus rejoiced greatly in the Holy Spirit. It is the same translation as in Zephaniah 3:17. The Greek agalliao, here translated as "rejoice," describes someone jumping for joy (G21). It is a compound word whose first part means "many," and the second part means "to jump." Here, too, movement is tamed in translation. Doesn't it fit our picture of the Lord that He is jumping for joy? Have we ever seen someone jump for joy? These are energetic movements. Would we call this a dance?

God, the Spirit, is already described as in intense movement at the beginning of the Scriptures. Genesis 1:2 says that the Spirit of God was hovering over the waters. The term "hover" means to remain in one place in the air. No energetic movements. However, the Hebrew rachaph, translated here as "hovering," has a meaning that actually expresses more movement (H7363): fluttering, whirring, vibrating, trembling, moving. The Spirit did not stay in one place in the air, but danced above the deep. There is intense movement at the beginning of the Bible.

Intense movement of God. Not a comprehensive doctrine, but evidence that God is in motion, not static. The statement that the Spirit trembles is consistent with the fact that light has a frequency of its own. God is light (1 John 1:5). Jesus is the light of the world (John 8:12). What is the frequency of the glory of God that we often see described in both the Old and New Testaments?

ACTIVATION 47:
EMOTION

Are you on the same wavelength as the actions of God described here? Intense movement? Have you ever felt intense emotion while creating something or when the work has been completed? Have you ever jumped for joy? For the same reason? Or have you ever experienced something so intense that you trembled inside? Are these emotions that you allow yourself to have in relation to your creativity or are they kept at bay? Do you let yourself be struck in the heart or do you tame what is going on to conform to current Christian norms, whatever those are?

> Take the time to pray about and to answer some or all of the questions and express them in your own creative language.

The Dance Of The Triune God

God determines when things happen. Everything has its time in the world (Eccl. 3:1 and 11). Jesus came into the world at God's appointed time (Gal. 4:4). Only God knows the end of the world, not even the Son (Matt. 24:36). God the Father determines what happens when and how. He determines individual steps and movements. So is He a choreographer? There are many layers.

Father, Son, and Spirit are described as the Trinity, a concept that is logically difficult to understand. It just does not work with the mind alone. The Church Fathers tried to describe this complexity with simple images. Gregory of Nazianzus, Archbishop of Constantinople and influential theologian, used the Greek verb perichoreo in the fourth century to describe the relationship between the three persons of God. It means dancing together, in a ring or a circle, around each other. Choros in Luke 15:25, describes the circle dances that were danced during the festival for the return of the prodigal son. Three hundred years later, Maximus the Confessor used the corresponding noun, perichoresis, for the first time to describe the interrelationship of the Father, the Son, and the Spirit (G. L. Prestige, 1964, 291). There is a lot of clever theological literature on this topic, which again complicates the whole thing. The Church Fathers, however, wanted to make it simple. Simply put, the three Persons of God move in an interwoven, perpetual dance, a concept that expresses one way of visualising the Trinity of God.

Add to that fact that the Father, Son, and Spirit are in motion in Scripture, in intense motion; then this explanation suits just fine. And it is easy to understand. The Creator in His plurality, so unlimited, creating from the fullness of Himself, is a dancer, One in motion with one another.

ACTIVATION 48:

DANCING TOGETHER

You are invited into this movement. What does that mean for you? John describes this interweaving, this dancing together in John 17:20-21 as a unity to which all followers of Jesus are invited. Do you accept this invitation? Do you experience it? Do you experience this dancing together in your creative process? What would have to happen for this experience to become deeper? To be expressed even more strongly in your art?

Take the time to pray about and to answer some or all of the questions and express them in your own creative language.

CHAPTER 9: BEYOND WHAT HAS ALREADY BEEN SAID

God as an artistic jeweller!

What else is God? I mean as an artist? Certainly, He is an artistic jeweller working with precious stones. In the description of God's throne room in Revelation 4, God Himself is compared in appearance to a jasper and a sardius. Jasper comes in red, yellow, brown or green. Sardius shimmers brown-red-orange. A rainbow is around the throne, shimmering like an emerald. It is interesting that the sign of His covenant, telling us we are protected and welcome, shines in God's throne room. And in front of the throne is a sea of glass. The original meaning of the Greek hualinos translated as glass, is "transparent as rain" (G5193). If one imagines the throne room with thunder and lightning (verse 5), flaming fire (same verse) and worship by the four living creatures and the 24 elders (verses 8-10), one can see that God is also a dramaturge.

An extraordinary one at that.

God created the being spoken of in Ezekiel 28:13 (NASB):

> "You were in Eden, the garden of God;
> Every precious stone was your covering:
> The ruby, the topaz and the diamond;
> The beryl, the onyx and the jasper;
> The lapis lazuli , the turquoise and the emerald;
> And the gold, the workmanship of your
> tambourines and flutes,
> Was in you.
> On the day that you were created
> They were prepared."

God speaks of beauty and splendour. The message is addressed to the king of Tyre, but it is largely interpreted as referring to God's adversary, who was cast out of Heaven. Originally, he was a creature created by an artist, adorned with precious stones, reflecting the creativity, beauty and splendour of his Creator. We as artists and in our art also reflect the creativity, beauty and splendour of God; we are invited to follow the ultimate artist wholeheartedly.

God also created the New Jerusalem. It is described in Revelation 21:2 as a bride adorned for her bridegroom. The city shines like a jewel, like a crystal-clear jasper (verse 11). It has twelve gates, each one pearl. The foundations of the city walls are adorned with precious stones: jasper, sapphire, chalcedony, emerald, sardonyx, sardius, chrysolite, beryl, topaz, chrysoprase, jacinth and amethyst. Whoever builds a city of pearls and precious stones, I will call an artistic jeweller.

ACTIVATION 49:

THE RADIANCE OF THE BRIDE

Look at the description of the bride, the New Jerusalem, with gates of pearls and foundations of precious stones. This city is so brightly agleam that it does not need a light source (Rev. 21:23) for the glory of God shines in it.

You are part of this bride (Eph. 5:32), i.e., your promise is that as part of the bride, you will be beautiful and spotless (Eph. 5:27), brightly agleam with God's glory. You should be perfect as your Father in heaven is perfect (Matt. 5:48).

In the here and now, are you already experiencing a glimmer, a glow, a radiance of that promise of the maturity of God's bride in your own life as an artist? Do you accept the value associated with this promise for yourself? The value that Jesus paid for on the cross?

> Take the time to pray about and to answer some or all of the questions and express them in your own creative language.

New Perspectives For Your Own Creativity

What changes did you experience when implementing the activations in this logbook? I hope that you have gained new perspectives on your own creativity that will help you to reach new shores on a basis which is deeper, more joyful, and more creative; to live from your creative identity and to be at home in your destiny. I pray that the things you have seen and learned will not be flashes in the pan, not beautiful mental buildings, but will lead you again and again into creative expressions and works for the glory of God and the spread of His kingdom. Very practical. Completely real. Totally natural.

Reflection

Did you reach your goal? If so, what changed? If not, why not?

What are the three most important statements about God as an artist for you?

What are the three most important messages about your own creativity?

What amazed you the most?

"The more I think about it, the more I feel there is nothing more artistic than loving people." Vincent van Gogh in a letter to his brother, Theo, September 18, 1888.

In this, in any case, God is unbeatable.
In this sense, too, He is the ultimate artist.